# Falling In Love With Me

## Loving Me

### By

### Yvonne Young

ISBN: 1-4107-9951-4 (e-book)
ISBN: 1-4107-9950-6 (Paperback)

Library of Congress Control Number:  2003097532


This book is printed on acid free paper.


Printed in the United States of America
Bloomington, IN

1stBooks - rev. 11/28/03

# DEDICATION

I dedicate this book to my daughter for being my sunshine and to my grandmother for she taught me how to love.

iv

# INTRODUCTION

I ask you all to please read this with an open heart. This book is targeted to every woman. The stay home mom, the college girl, corporate executive, part-time worker-come-home-just-in-time-for-the-kids, teacher, bricklayer, bus driver, taxi driver, chef, fashion designer, model, actress, producer, meteorologist, doctor, lawyer, clown, gymnast, politician,store clerk, service representative, janitor, nurse, archaeologist, engineer, computer specialist, stripper, business owner, evangelist, missionary, prostitute, soldier. Some of the things you are about to read you may already do. But, I guarantee you that none of you do all these things. The key to success after reading is to keep this book with you wherever you go. A place where you can pick it up and take a glimpse when you need that extra umph, high five or friendly reminder to get you through that existing challenge. Also, another key to success after reading this book is to do all the things I suggest with an open mind and non-biased opinion. Most importantly, read this book with love in your heart, free from animosity that the world wants to give you. Let it all go.

Okay, take a deep breathe and let's begin. Look in the mirror, because you are about to fall in love.

# 1

# DON'T LET SURPRISES SURPRISE YOU

There will always be dinners to be cooked, laundry to be done, beds to be made and houses to clean. Every day brings new demands. There are only 24 hours before the next day filled with demands begins all over. But, why do do get stressed when the kids call us as soon as we get home or someone asks us to do something that was not on the agenda? Why did we let the car in front of us that was going only 25 mph give us the headache that we still have six hours later? Did we think everyone's schedule evolved around ours, just because we left the house too late? Do we expect everyone on the Interstate to speed frantically to work like we do? The answer is yes!

Then someone walks in the job and asks us to do something that just doesn't fall in line with our schedule. Before we know it we are frustrated and complaining. Why did we ever think everything at our job would fall in line with our schedule? It sounds pretty amazing, but judging by our reactions we simply expect this. The world is not our stopwatch. So when someone walks in and surprises you at work with a really big demand, just accept it. Be determined to stay calm and poised. Don't let your brain think irrationally about leaving or starting your own business. That takes careful planning and preparation. Many of us have bills to pay and families to take care of. Plain and simple, you need that next paycheck.

Be determined to stay calm and poised. You will be in a better frame of mind to handle the task. Realize that this is how life works. Life is full of surprises, good times, bad times, disappointments and rewards. It usually takes patience to get the rewards, especially the ones worth keeping. It is an ongoing process. The key to peace on a daily basis is not to let the surprises surprise you! You can get through it! When surprises come, make a conscious effort to breathe slowly in and out and think, "Calm down, you can handle this." But you have to really mean it and you have to remember to feel and say this right in the middle of the crises. This will take constant effort. If you really think about it, it's really not that bad. Things truly could always be worse, and they will be if you keep letting little things stress you. Just relax.

This is the perfect opportunity for you to dig down within yourself and get to know you. This is when you find out what you are made of. I believe that you can and will do it! I know you can! I know I can! Don't let this hourly demand take your control away and worry you for the rest of your day that is currently perfect. Don't let this one circumstance make you treat friends and family in an unloving way. Don't let this circumstance give you a zit that will last the next three days. It will only be harder for you to overcome the next surprise. Because, believe me its coming!

The world is forever changing but your effort in trying to stay calm, forgiving the driver in front of you and helping your co-worker one day. Think about it: in the beginning you were late going to work. Just realize it was your fault that you were late and not the driver in front of you. Make a change and start your day off in a more organized fashion. Stay calm and remember this too will pass. So now the surprises are not surprises anymore! Just unwanted, expected situations that you can handle CALMLY!

"If the worm doesn't deal with being slow and squirmy he will never see how it feels to fly and be beautiful."

Yvonne

4

**2**

# SMOOTH, SOFT AND SURE

It is very important to feel good underneath the clothes and make-up. It is very important to feel feminine and like a lady even if you don't consider yourself the prissy type. It is very important for you to look good, not just for a man, or for other women you compete with, for your job, but for you. Respecting and feeling good about yourself is most important. Once you do this everything else submits, because you don't look good based on circumstances anymore. This way you are consistent in looking and feeling good. First, women are women and men are men, there is a major difference and it should stay that way. I am not trying to tell you how to dress, but am suggesting that your body speak, "Femininity." Feminine is defined in the American Heritage College Dictionary as characterized by or possessing qualities generally attributed to a woman. So please don't build up a defensive wall. I am simply asking you to be what you are.

Okay, back to the subject. First, shave. Keep, the under arm "dips smooth." Pits is yuck, so let's get away from that word. Let us leave the arm hair and the pit word for the men, and hopefully that won't be excessive either. But, that's another book. The prickly arm hairs are a definite No No. Even a little is yuck. It takes only 30 seconds to shave them.

Second, keep the legs nice and smooth in the winter and summer. A really great disposable shave that is great for daily shaving and soft to the skin is by BIC its less that $3. Its topped with Vitamin E and gives a pretty smooth shave; the name is BIC Plus and it comes in aqua packaging. Whether you are married, in a relationship dating or just floating solo this is not for your spouse, boyfriend or confidant, but for YOU! Three, keep the finger nails and toe nails clipped and painted. I prefer clear, it's classy, simple and beautiful, but pick the color that you like best. Now for the women wo do the professional manicure, you already have that taken care of, but for the women who don't this is an easy step for you. I think clear speaks a lot. It says, "I shine." You can shine if you believe it in your mind. Most importantly, you have to believe that you shine everyday. Even if sometimes someone else is in the spotlight one day. This doesn't dim your shine. It just brightens the entire room! If one day it rains or something is happening terrible in your life, it is your spirit that makes you, not the world, you don't have to stay on the emotional roller coaster by letting circumstances dictate the woman that you strive to be!

Forth, shaving the bikini line is not optional all year round and for the rest of the "Forget Me Not" area (that's what we'll call it). Hey, we're creating some female jargon that's more appropriate. You just shave it like a brand new baby. You will look and feel better after you shower. Seeing a soft smooth body will definitely boost your confidence and sex appeal. Go ahead and do a little dance. If you're married, your husband will love it too. But, remember, you are doing this for you and no one else. Also, just before stepping out of the shower a lightly scented body wash works great. There are many for sensitive skin for the women who are sensitive to perfumes. I still feel soap works better for soft friction in cleansing the body and the body wash is a great second step. It's a wonderful feeling getting out of the shower with smooth skin from head to toe, nice finger and toe nails glistening and the body softly expressing soft sentiments in the air. Dove soap is wonderful. Also, pick a body lotion with Vitamin E, It's great for the skin. Vaseline makes an awesome one that is fragrance free and great for the skin. It absorbs so nicely and makes you so so soft. These are all inexpensive easy ways that all take less than an hour for you to make yourself feel good all day.

On your way to work whether you are covered in long johns, a short fitting skirt, stretch-fitting shirt, big sweatshirt or sexy bathing suit on a hot summer day, YOU know that your body is well groomed and you feel wonderful! You feel feminine! You feel like a true lady! You can even smell the soft scent on your body as you gracefully walk across the floor. Even the guy in the elevator notices your natural confidence and can smell the soft mysterious lovely scent, but you don't even notice how cute he is and him admiring you because you are caught up in life. Your are caught up in getting to learn how to love yourself! You are caught up in getting to know you a little bit better. If he wants to admire you, let him go ahead and you didn't have to do one thing to taunt or tease him!

Later on during the day you sit in your chair and rub your skin and feel you soft body and think, "I AM ONE HECK OF A WOMAN, YEA A GOOD WOMAN, A SEXY WOMAN, A BEAUTIFUL WOMAN, YES THAT'S ME!"

"The person I want to be like is a better, loving me…"

Yvonne

# 3

# NO MORE LOOSE CHANGE

How many times have you dug and dug through your purse on the way to work, holding up traffic at the stop light looking for your lipstick, parking tag, or that friend's number that you know that you put in the night before. Then for the next 60 seconds you stress out, only to find it in the bottom of your bag or on the bathroom sink when you return home that evening. Worrying never helped you find it, and it only creates energy that transforms to stress. This lesson will be one of the easiest things you can do to decrease the levels of unnecessary stress you create in your day. Every purse usually has a little side zip. If not, buy one that does or buy an additional change purse. This is the area where you want to keep some of the smallest most important things you own. Things that you can find in your purse immediately. Like a pen when you need to sign that credit slip at the retail counter. Also, in this zipper you want to keep some change, at least two dollar's worth. This will leave enough money for toll road or extra change for the lunch you just purchased that cost $6.17.

Keep your lipstick or lip gloss there for touch-ups throughout the day. And for the days you forget your lipstick, keep an extra tube at work. This way you won't go through your day feeling ugly. You know usually no one else notices as much about yourself as you do. But, what's most important is how you feel about yourself, and if lipstick and a splash of color does that then that's great. But remember what you feel in your heart is what makes you stay beautiful after you wipe or kiss the lipstick away.

Next, keep a safety pin. On those days when a button comes off that $300 suit we race around asking everyone or run to the nearest drug store, only to set our schedule back another 30 minutes, adding more stress to our day.

Last but not least, we need to always keep the tampon or panty liner in our purse. Some of you know the day, hour and minute when mensee will come. For others, our mensee makes her own decision and we can never tell. Then we forget to stuff our purse with the necessities in the middle of the mensee and then go to the bathroom only to find that the stupid machine is empty. The only thing that is available are the maxi pads that are as thick as a pamper!

13

"How dare the company forget to stock the machine!" We bang on it and start our search to the nearest friend or store. Please, just keep one in there at all times. There are pocket ones and neatly wrapped liners. Its all about being prepared for the mishaps. We can't be prepared for the big ones. But for our sake we can prepare for the small. Just imagine digging in your purse in the line at the grocery store counter, walking to lunch as we bump into the person we haven't seen in five years and go right to the side pocket without even looking and grabbing just what we need. Now that's a lady's perfection.

We got security right in our purse pocket!


"Your big problem is only a bunch of little problems you continued to neglect"

Yvonne

# 4

# H20 YOUR WORRIES AWAY

This will change the way you drink water for the rest of your life. This step is the easiest but one of the most critical steps in the book. It's not simply you doing this crucial step, but HOW you do it!

Drink a glass of water first thing in the morning and a glass of water at night. Drink only the filtered or spring water, because there have been way too many studies showing toxins left in our tap water. I know you are thinking, "Okay this lady is making money telling me to drink water, this is insane!" But, drinking is not the key, it's how you drink it. First thing, when you wake up go to your kitchen and get your pure water. Next, find a quiet room in your home, where you won't be disturbed, and sit on the floor. Clear your mind of all past and future thoughts. Don't think about what you didn't complete last night or that your child was up all night with the coughs or that your best friend stated she saw your husband with a beautiful woman that was probably just a good friend. This is your time for you. This is the time where you nourish yourself. This is the time that you feel your true beauty within. Now lift your glass slowly and drink, non stop. Think these thoughts, "I AM BEAUTIFUL. I AM HAPPY. I

HAVE PEACE." Say this 3 times. Feel the cold water drift slowly down your throat and feel the cool sensation in your stomach. Allow only pure happy thoughts within and then slowly breathe in and out. Just in that time you have undergone a defense mechanism for today's, "Have Tos and Hurries."

Now at the end of the dayafter you have undergone all of the demands of the day and made it through what you thought you could not, go to the frig and get that pure glass of water and find that quiet place again. Get on the floor. And by the way, the reason for lowering yourself to the floor is to humble yourself. We must remember we are better than no one else. We are not the only people in this world that bad things happen to. The Creator owes us nothing, because none of us are perfect. We have all been bad girls and boys at times. This time you drink the water for a different purpose, to cleanse your spirit! Your day may have been great, but don't let down your spiritual guard of peace because a crazy day is on its way or, what you think to be, the worst day of your life. Don't fret, because a great day is on its way. Change is the only thing that's constant. Remember our first chapter? Expect the unexpected. You have to be determined not to live in fear. Just know whatever it is, you can overcome it as long as you keep that inner harmony. Okay, now drink, drink, slowly drink. Feel all the past worries of the day wiped away. That fight with your husband, best friend or co-worker. That thoughtless comment or response you made today. That big piece of cake you ate that killed your diet. That zit that no one else saw. Let it go, let the water take it away. Now say, "I LEARN. I FORGET. I CAN." Say this 3 times. Cleanse your soul. Stop living in the past. It's in the past. Stop letting it fester and making you age more quickly, and eating up that beautiful spirit you have. Just drink, learn and forget. Feel the restoration. Feel the process. Feel the cleansing. Feel you. You are not your circumstances. You are the foundation in this crazy life. Your life can't shake you because you have inner peace. You have faith. You have you. No one or no situation can take that away!

"Only look back if you are stretching your neck"

Yvonne

# 5

# GET OUT OF CONTROL

So many times we worry about things we have no control over. Don't get me wrong, organization, planning, and improvement should be a continual process. But, the things that are out of your control you simply have to let them go. So, the easiest way for solving this problem is to feel comfortable with uncontrollable situations.

What I am about to ask you to do will be one of the silliest things you have ever done. But, it will also be one of the most effective things you have ever done. For this one you need some open space. This time I want you to do 21 jumping-jacks with your eyes closed. Of course exercise is great medicine for stress and activity burns calories, but this exercise won't get you from a size 10 to a size 3, but it will definitely get you up when you just feel too lazy to do the dishes or that last minute task before going to bed. But mainly, it will allow you to feel okay about not being in control and be happy about it!

When you do the jump in jacks you close your eyes, breathe in and out and count. 1, 2, 3, 4 and so on. Now as you do this you will start to become unstable and won't stay in the same place as you do your jumping jacks. And don't you dare try to stay in control! Just let your body go where it must and think how good it feels not to be in control. You will start to laugh and feel even sillier, just like you were when you were a kid with no worries and cares. Feel that way, find the little kid inside and let it out. Produce those aging defensive cells.

How are you doing? Is it killing you to do this? Did the last thing you stressed over that you knew you couldn't control kill you? Evidently not, because you are reading this book. Maybe you feel you just can't make it through some terrible situation you are in right now. But if you have breath in your body that means you have just enough time to get up and make a positive change. Now this is a great exercise to do with your kids and to teach them the concept. You can also do this with your spouse. This will teach the family to enjoy each other when things come up that you can't control. Do this with your girlfriends. Learn to laugh in the midst of bad times. Hey, some things may be out of control, but at least you can look good. Why be ugly and mad? Feel good about life! You are out of control

and I can do nothing with you.  Are you going through something?
Yes, you are going right THROUGH IT!


"A rock doesn't have to sink in the pond when you throw
it.  If you throw it the right way it will skip right across."

Yvonne

**6**

**MISTAKES 101**

Take Advantage of this class. When has there ever been a time that we can take classes that directly apply to our family, career and everyday living? Never! How many times have we taken classes in the future and wondered, "When will I ever use this?" Algebra, geography, chemistry, history, I didn't feel as though any of my classes were applicable to everyday life until I started graduate school. That took over 22 years! But, then came mistakes 101. This class is FREE and the teacher is you! You just can't get much better than this. But, you can still fail this class. If you take this class and after each lesson or mistake you look back and play it over and over in your mind then you earn an F! If after each lesson or mistake you beat yourself and say, "You are just a terrible person!" Then you receive a D because you thought you were too perfect to make a mistake in the first place and no one is perfect. If after a mistake or lesson you just feel sad and do nothing or think nothing, then you receive a C. At least you aren't evil because you have remorse and want to do better. If you make a mistake and say, "I will do better next time," and just don't seize the next opportunity, then you receive a B. Girl, you almost got it, because you are learning to get back up after you fall. You are developing some stamina. I always support stamina in my lady sisters.

Now let's talk about how to get that A! How can you move to the head of the class and become the teacher's pet? Remember you are the teacher and now you will love the best student, who is also you. That means, yeah you got it, you love you! You feel good about You! Now after that mistake or lesson you feel bad. This is natural and and person who has good intentions should feel bad. But the key is not to let that feeling fester and produce unnecessary stress. Secondly, think on it just for a little while and figure out the root of the mistake. Then take that root and pluck it up. Don't let it grow into the same mistake again. After you figure out the root just simply decide that you won't do it that way anymore and think how you will do it differently. If it is something small just make the promise to yourself. If it is big then write it down and make a plan on how you should do it. Ask an honest person and someone you can trust if you need company or advice. Please don't get advice from someone who will just throw it in your face if you fall again. Don't seek advice from someone who will just give you the,"he said, she said, and yeah I heard this and that." This is all nonsense and we need to get that type of conversation out of our lives. All of us need some help at some point. No one ever succeeded at anything alone.

After you figure out how you can do it better next time, be happy you made the mistake. Yes, I did say be happy. I didn't say be happy before you made it and do it anyway. And I didn't say be happy that you made the mistake if you didn't learn from it! I said after you figured out that you can do better, be happy. Bravo! You just passed Mistake 101 with flying colors, a free class in life where you are the teacher and the student. It's a class that directly applies to you. A class that results in a stronger and better person. Now you can be real with yourself and know that you are not perfect. You make mistakes. You will make more. But you are growing and you are becoming a better and improved person everyday! I am so proud of you! I am proud of me because I am learning, too, by writing these heart felt words to you. Thanks for lending me your ear and being my book friend. I sincerely mean it and appreciate you taking the time to read this. The only reason I write these words to you is because these are things I have struggled with too. I know how it feels to be your worst critic. Hey, but that's okay because we all have things we need to do better.

"If you MISS the TAKE while acting out your life, just do it again until you get it right. Then record it so you won't forget how you did it."

Yvonne

*Yvonne Young*

# 7

# TAKE TIME TO DO NOTHING

Just before going to bed you need to have time that you do nothing. Absolutely nothing. This is a time where you don't think on what you did during the day. This is a time where you don't think on what you have to do tomorrow. There is a quote from the Bible that says, "Therefore do not worry about tomorrow, for tomorrow will worry about its own things. Sufficient for the day is its own trouble." This scripture is so full of wisdom and very applicable to our lives. Why do we spend so much energy on worries of tomorrow when sometimes we have just enough energy for what we are doing at that very moment. So this is the time for you to be free. You need to free yourself from your ambitions, plans for tomorrow, your mistakes, your accomplishments, your assets, your bills, your friends, your enemies. Take the time to just breathe. All you have to do is find a quiet room, one that speaks peace and tranquility. One that you can feel at ease in. This may be the bathroom. As you walk to take this sit down, breathe slowly in and out. You have to prepare yourself and let go all of the demands of your life. Remember if you don't have your health or stable frame of mind you are no good to do all the things you want to do. Remember to love you sometimes. Its not selfish. You are creating a better person for your family and friends. If you are any thing like me you spend lots of time inspiring and sending little cards, books, letters, hugs and kisses to friends to uplift them. Then you might find yourself longing to receive the same, not because you feel you deserve it but because you would just like to feel that loved sometimes, too. But, they don't do the same for you because they assume that you are the strong one. The one that can get through it all! If you think about it, you did portray this image to your friends and family. Showing that you can "multi-task" like no other. You always smile and seem like you are on top of the world. If only you would have taken time to cry on someone's shoulder and let them know you are human too, they would have given you the love you need. So stop frontin: You need people too.

Okay so back to walking to the quiet room. You are walking and slowly breathing in and out. You are training your mind to let go of it all. You are telling your muscles and nerves to relax because they will have no work to do. You are slowly traveling to your innermost being. You are feeling your heart and soul. Wow, you didn't even know you could find the place and that it would feel so good. You suddenly realize that all the things you were seeking in all the vacations, wine, sex and that big bowl of Haagan Dazs was right in your heart. This really feels good. Now that you are in that neutral state of mind, just breath in and out, very slow, and feel the oxygen enter your body that our plants have prepared so naturally for us. Feel the carbon dioxide flow out and feel how your body naturally purifies itself, only if you would let it. Stop intoxicating your body with worries. So many times we hear doctors speak of the toxins we feed ourselves. Some of the most deadly toxins are the thoughts we allow to enter and grow in our mind. You have control on what enters your body, and the best way to stop those terrible thoughts is to keep peace within. Allow yourself to travel within and just rest and breath in your soul. The world will always have some type of judgment and chaos. But the peace you have within, no one can take that away if you take a stand and just be. Just be still…

"I go in to get away."

Yvonne

# 8

# MAKE A NOT TO DO LIST

How many times have we heard from scholars and successful people say, "WRITE DOWN YOUR GOALS AND YOU WILL SEE GREAT RESULTS" MAKE A PLAN FOR WHAT YOU WANT TO DO WITH YOUR LIFE!" Yes, that is wonderful advice and I apply that to my life also. But, its equally important to write down the things you don't want to do anymore. How many times do we find ourselves trying very hard NOT to do something again. Then under pressure we become angry or anxious and end up conducting ourselves the same way. Then beat ourselves up for it. It is easy to say we aren't going to do something. But, it is hard being under pressure when someone catches you when you least expect it, or perhaps is plain rude to you, or gives you some of the worst news in your life Its very hard to be peaceful in the midst of a storm. But this is the first step. We need to write down the things we don't want to do anymore. These should be habits that you have been trying to break, but just can't seem to break them. These are things that after you do them, you worry and beat yourself up over for the next hour of even couple of days. These are the things that you know if you could stop doing you would be a better mother, co-worker, wife or friend. These are the things that are important to you and the people you love. These are the things centered around the values you grew up on. These are not the things you do just to prove something to the world. If that's the case then one of the things on your list should be "stop trying to prove myself to everyone!" It's okay; we all go through that one, whether we want to admit it or not. Don't make your list to lengthy and don't be too hard on yourself. But I do want to give you the first and the last thing on your list. Okay, number one for everyone is don't give up and the last thing on your list will be don't go to sleep with anger on your heart for anyone. (I heard a speaker at a business seminar state, "The average millionaire has applied for bankruptcy 2.5 times. That is amazing.) The key to success is making mistakes and not letting them stop you. That first one focuses on you and the last one focuses on the people you love. I know we have all tried this. But, tell me this, "Have we all done this?" NO! Having peace with ourselves and the people we care about the most causes us to be happy within. I encourage you to go to some of the most important people in your life (your spouse, children, parents, best friend, etc.) Ask them, "If there is one thing you could request that I stop doing what would it be?" You will be amazed how important it is to just stop doing the little nagging things;

it will change your relationships! If your husband says, "Stop nagging me so much!" Don't get mad just stop nagging him so much. If he says, "Stop going to your mom's so much," that's something you all need to talk about. Maybe he wants more of your attention, maybe its something else. But come to a fair agreement. If your best friend says, "Stop eating so healthy." Don't stop eating healthy just don't be obsessed with it. Keep treating your body right and be proud of it. When you go to your kids, take to heart what they say. Responses like this from children are free of bias and judgment. We can learn so much from their sincerity and the total dependence of a child. I love you and am rooting for you. Are you rooting for me? Let all women encourage each other! We all go through many of the same things no matter what our physical make-up is. If we would only be real with ourselves and happy with ourselves, we could treat each other so much better.

"Some of the biggest mistakes in life made us be the amazing people we are today."

Yvonne

# 9

# CATCH YOUR OWN EYE

P lease don't do it! Don't you dare play that slow song that makes you think about how good it feels to hurt. Don't play the song that makes you think of the man last year - if you had only let him talk or if you had only not said that last comment, or... No just stop holding on to the past. Because if he really cared about who you are, the true person you are, he would have called you back or made an attempt to spend time. If he really wanted you he would have made the time. Think about it, how many men have you told, "I am so sorry, I have been so busy." But, then when you met that hottie in the middle of lunch or in between those two tasks. You made that call. See, you make time for what you really want. And he would too. You wouldn't have had to initiate. Think about it; this guy isn't perfect, either. He made mistakes and didn't you overlook them? Shouldn't he do the same? Why do we feel we lose so much when that so-called special person walks out of our life? Why did we anticipate some phone calls that never came? Why do we spend countless minutes thinking of woulda, couldas instead of thinking cana, willas?

Learn and move on. Realize just the wonderful person that you are. Improve upon yourself. Carry yourself and walk with respect and the person that is meant for you will recognize and discover you. Be pretty for you. Keep your house clean for you. Get that body massage for you. Get your hair done for you. Let him call. Let him ask you for the next date. Don't get me wrong; it is year 2003 and yes women are independent. Believe me, I know about being the superwoman. Single mom, graduate student, broker, community helper, God seeker and all of the above can be hard to do simultaneously. I know some men like aggressive women. But, sometimes we need to be real with ourselves and know that a lot of times we try a little too hard. A lot of times it evolves around our own insecurities about ourselves. We get lonely during the evening and end up calling that guy we know isn't our type. During the date we think of how uncomfortable we feel and how we are afraid people may make associations about who we are because of the person we are with. First, you should never have made the call. Second, you shouldn't care about what people think. What about what you think? Get home and find the root. Ask yourself what made you make the call. Find the feelings that started this. This way, when you are feeling lonely again you won't end up making the same mistake again. So after the date, we always expect the call, whether we want the call or not. We get caught up thinking "He should feel privileged I asked him out and he didn't even call me after our date!" We end up chasing something we don't want anyway just to get the last word just to prove a point. In the end we feel pretty small.

Ask yourself, "Why did I call in the first place?" What was so wrong with picking up a good book to read? Not a love story either. One that is centered around character and happiness. What is wrong with taking a long hot bubblebath or just running in the park? And if you feel like you would never do those things, ask yourself, "Is it because of your insecurity or pride?" If it isn't then find out what it is. If you were all that you wouldn't be alone anyway. So get over yourself or get real with yourself. So many times we think too little or too much of ourselves. We should use this time just being ourselves. Stop evaluating every single thing that you do. Sometimes we can get a big head. There is always someone prettier, more fit. Pretty can catch a man, but pretty can't keep one! It's only you that makes you. No one else can give your mate that. Be the best at that and nothing else. That is all you can be and be proud doing it. Is it so bad to check out a movie by yourself or to go to the local bookstore for a poetry reading? Maybe you would have met your future husband in that same environment, the guy that is out alone because he has no girlfriend that he is cheating on. The guy who is fit or educated because he is at the park or local poetry reading.

Just be you and you will find someone like you. Be a better you. Take care of your body. Take care of your heart. Read and restore your soul. Eat Right. Hold your head up. Impress yourself. Look in the mirror and fall in love with the person you been neglecting all your life. Finally, when you see another female who is wearing that short skirt or is flirting a little too much or is drawing way much too attention to herself, PLEASE, don't talk about her, don't hate. Remember things about yourself that you have to improve upon and give her some love and encouragement. Do the unthinkable and smile and say, "Hi!"

"There is never a true exit.  The door always leads to somewhere else.  Stop trying to run away."

Yvonne

# 10

# TOO MUCH OF A GOOD THING IS BAD

Tor this one I am talking about FOOD. How many times have we decided that we would stick to a diet and do good for ten hours of the day or five days of the week, only to pig out that night or that weekend and sleep on it. Remember it's not who starts out fast at the sound of the gun. It's who paces themselves, endures and finishes. It's all about discipline and calming down. When you get home don't run to the cupboard and grab a bag of chips because of the boss that just made you mad or the kids that are running around like crazy. Grab a cold glass of water and just take a moment for YOU. Reason with yourself. Take a deep breath and cleanse out those frustrations. So many times I have munched on Teddy grahams and Wow Potato chips, not because I was hungry but because I was thinking of something that happened that day and before I know it half of the bag is gone and then next day my pants fit a little bit tighter. I know you say, "I understand what I need to do, but doing it is something completely different!"

So there is one simple answer to this question-**Snack Cups**. It sounds silly, but this will help you lose weight like no other diet! Promise that you will never eat directly out of a big bag or big box.

This is the way to wide hips, tight pants, poppy stomachs and regrets, "I shouldn't have eaten that." Here's what you do. Go to the store and get some 4 ounce dishes. You can get tupperware or snack bags. I purchased some really cute porcelain dishes with strawberries on them. It encourages me because they are so cute. My weakness was cereal. I would go all day and eat healthy low carb meals, only to eat handfuls of cereal straight out of the box late at night, which is terrible because I was sleeping on it. Now, I put my cereal in my snack cup and that is all I eat. You can put your candy, ice cream, cookies, crackers, pudding, yogurt in these little cups. You will slowly see your body trim down if you are consistent. This way you aren't cutting out the things you love. We women work too hard at too many things not to treat ourselves. Just don't punish yourselves treating yourselves. Go ahead, take one piece of bread off the sandwich or cut it in half. Take away 10 french fries. Spoon off some of those mashed potatoes. Cut that piece of cake in half. So many times we only eat the food because its there. Its already packaged that way, so we think we should eat it all. Now I don't want you to waste food. There are too many homeless people out here for that. Just don't put it on your plate, or when you have to go for fast food, don't get the french fries. Just buy the sandwich. Many times we over eat because of unhappiness or stress. We have to find this within and not in food. Before you pick up that junk, grab that glass of water and let all the worries go. Grab your snack cup, and the next week zip up those pants and say, "Yeah, Baby!"

"I lose weight by eating a little of lots of things I love!"

Yvonne

# 11

# YOU WRITE THIS ONE

This is the most important part of my book. This is the part where you tell me what you would like my next book to be about in 20 words or less. My next book will be centered around what all my readers want. Remember, I am doing this for us women. I want us to feed off of each other's positive energy and encouragement. The next book should be out within the next year. Also, I will send you an e-mail response that I received it. I may also ask your permission if I could use your words as a quote with your name and area you are from. This would only be with your permission of course! Please e-mail to YesWomenWin@aol. com

Remember take this book with you wherever you go. Take notes in the back as you progress and work to be consistent. I hope you feel better, look better and live better. But, most importantly, I hope you now love the person you see every morning in the mirror or at least learning to. That person will be with you through thick and thin you may as well make a habit of enjoying her company.


I love All of you!

Yvonne

## ABOUT THE AUTHOR

Yvonne Young is a 27 year old single mom who has a Bachelor of Science Degree in Business, Series 7 License and Life & Health Insurance License as a Broker in a large VA Firm and a current MBA student at a local university in Richmond VA. Yvonne has worked very hard and wants everyone to know the key to her endurance is spiritual guidance, family and faith. She has felt at times that she wanted to give up because of life's disappointments, but never did. She only wants to encourage other women to do the same. She also wants to communicate the importance of encouragement and love communicated between all women.

Yvonne has many goals she wishes to pursue in the future and are currently working on. But, emphasises the importance of goals, but most importantly, appreciating the "Now" in life. Being content is a key to day to day peace and without a good state of mind nothing can be accomplished. She wishes every woman love, health, happiness, peace and prosperity.

www.ingramcontent.com/pod-product-compliance
Lightning Source LLC
Chambersburg PA
CBHW050335290526
45785CB00006B/2504